W9-AYR-618

| DATE DUE | | | |
|---|---|---|---|
| | | | |
| | | | |
| | | | |
| | | | |
| | | | |
| | | | |
| | | | |
| | | | |
| | | | |
| | | | |
| | | | |
| | | | |
| | | | |

# PAINTERS

## THE PERFORMERS

Laura Conlon

The Rourke Press, Inc.
Vero Beach, Florida 32964

Edited by Sandra A. Robinson

PHOTO CREDITS
All photos © Kyle Carter

**Library of Congress Cataloging-in-Publication Data**

Conlon, Laura, 1959-
    Painters / Laura Conlon.
    p.  cm. — (The Performers discovery library)
    Includes index.
    ISBN 1-57103-065-4
    1. Painting—Vocational guidance—Juvenile literature.
[1. Artists. 2. Vocational guidance. 3. Occupations.]  I. Title.
II. Series.
ND1146.C59   1994
750'.23—dc20
                                    94-11602
                                    CIP
                                    AC

**Printed in the USA**

# TABLE OF CONTENTS

# PAINTERS

Painters are people who use paints to create pictures. Some of their pictures show what the painter sees. Other paintings show something that the painter has imagined.

Painters make pictures by putting paint on a surface of some kind. Cloth and paper are common surfaces. Thousands of years ago, the earliest painters painted on the walls of caves.

Painters are often called "artists." Several other groups of creative people, such as **sculptors,** are also types of artists.

*A painter is an artist who creates pictures by painting onto a surface*

## KINDS OF PAINTERS

Painters are sometimes grouped by their painting "style." For example, artists who paint scenes that look very real, paint in a "realistic" style. Their paintings look like what they see.

**Commercial** painters are hired to paint pictures for books, newspapers, magazines and greeting cards. "Fine" artists paint mostly for themselves to create something that is beautiful.

*In a realistic style of her own, fine artist Peg McNamara paints wild birds*

# LEARNING TO BE A PAINTER

Like most artists, painters are born with a special talent. They have the ability to paint the things they see or imagine. Studying other artists' paintings and ways to paint helps young painters develop their own style and sharpen their skills.

Most artists study art in classes. After high school art classes, young painters can take art classes in college. They can also attend an art school or study painting privately with teachers who are skilled painters.

*Young painters learn to improve their skills with the help of art teachers*

## WHAT PAINTERS PAINT

A painter's subject matter — what an artist paints — is limited only by his or her imagination. Painters never run out of subjects!

Many painters paint the things they find most interesting. A painter may have a special interest in people, the sea, historical events, religious figures, dogs, airplanes or wildlife.

Many commercial painters paint whatever they are hired to paint. They may paint a mountain scene one day and a sailing ship the next.

11

*This artist paints a scene from a photo*

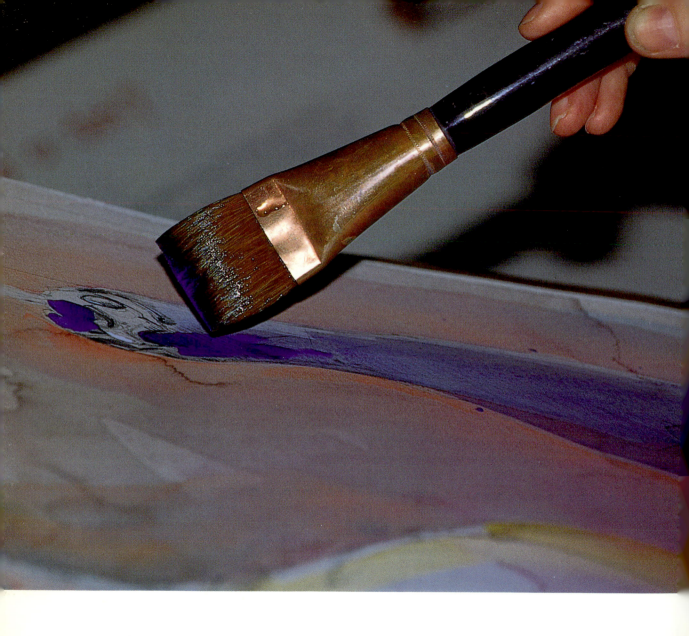

An artist's broad brush strokes in blue become a peacock's neck

*Ms. McNamara's brush gives life and color to birds she paints from exhibits in the Field Museum of Chicago, Illinois*

## MAKING A PAINTING

Young painters usually try using many different types of painting and paints. Three of the best-known types of paint are oil, watercolor and acrylic.

Oil paints are most often used on a fabric or **canvas** surface. Watercolors work best on paper. Acrylic paints can be used on many surfaces.

Some painters draw their ideas in pencil or ink before they paint them. This is called **sketching.** Leonardo da Vinci, a famous artist of long ago, made hundreds of sketches for just one painting!

14

*An artist sketches a fishing boat before painting it*

## THE PAINTER'S WORKPLACE

The painter's workplace is wherever the artist paints. Painters often work in home **studios.** Studios are places where artists keep their paints, paintings and an **easel** or drawing table.

Painters may work at fairs, shops or museums where their work is on display. They may also work "on location" to paint a scene, often in the outdoors.

*An artist with her easel "on location" in England*

# THE PAINTER'S TOOLS

A painter may use several "tools" to make a painting. One is the **palette,** a thin board or tray. Artists spread each paint color they want to use onto the palette.

The painter dips into the paint with a brush. Brushes come in many shapes and sizes. Most are made of animal hair.

A painter also uses special "knives" to mix paints. Artists can also use these knives to add paint to a surface.

*Ms. McNamara dips a brush into watercolors held in the trays of her palette*

## IN THE GALLERY

The goal of many fine artists is to have their paintings shown in a **gallery.** Galleries are stores that display and sell works of art.

A painter shows some of his or her paintings to a gallery owner. The owner may then decide to exhibit, or show, the artist's work.

People visit galleries to look at and buy paintings. Some paintings by famous artists sell for thousands — or even millions — of dollars.

*Galleries show and sell paintings by fine artists*

## CAREERS IN PAINTING

Finding a full-time career as a painter is difficult. Many people would like to paint for a living. However, the number of people who actually buy paintings, or hire artists, is small.

Painters often paint on a part-time basis. They may find other work in the field of art. Many painters, for example, give private lessons, and teach art in schools and colleges. A few painters own galleries.

## Glossary

**canvas** (KAN vuhs) — rough cloth stretched over a frame and used by painters

**commercial** (kuh MUR shul) — referring to work that is done to earn money

**easel** (EE zul) — a frame that supports an artist's canvas or another painting surface

**gallery** (GAL er ee) — a place for showing and selling paintings

**palette** (PAL uht) — a thin board or tray that a painter uses to hold and mix dabs of paint

**sculptor** (SKULPT er) — an artist who shapes works of art from rocks, clay or some other material

**sketching** (SKETCH ing) — the act of making a quick, simple drawing

**studio** (STOO dee o) — a room where an artist paints